First Printing, 2018
Wild Cabbage Books
wildcabbagebooks.com

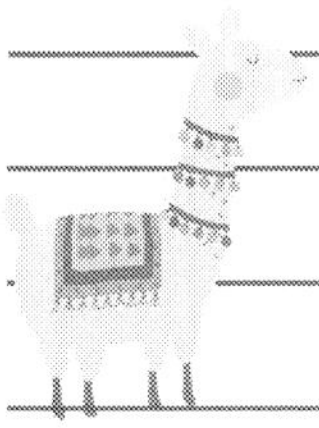

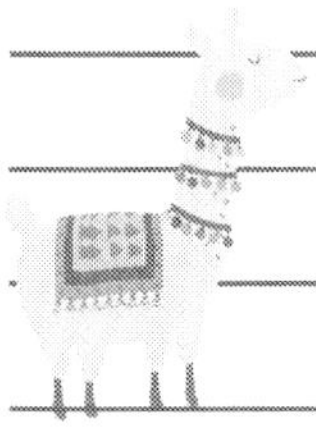

Each of us is limitless; each of us with his or her right upon the earth.

– Walt Whitman

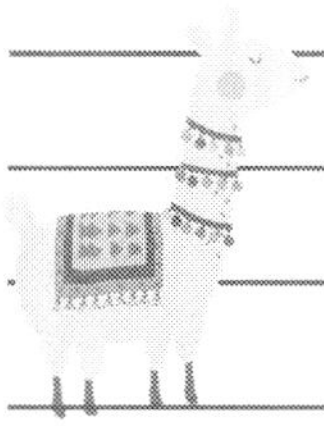

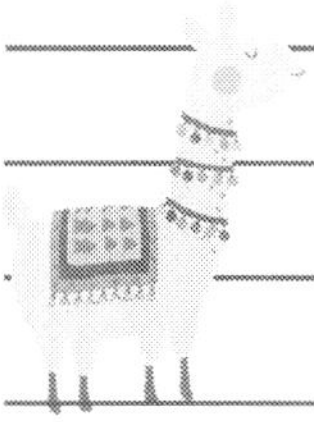

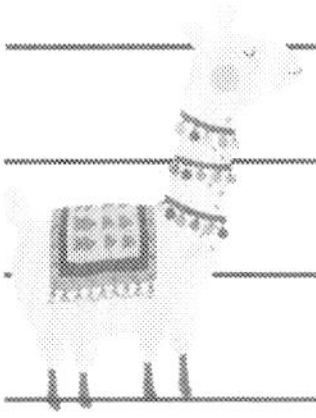

This above all: to thine ownself be true.

– Shakespeare

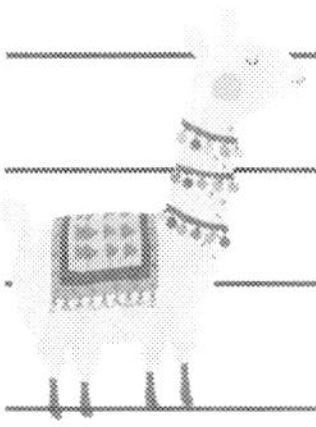

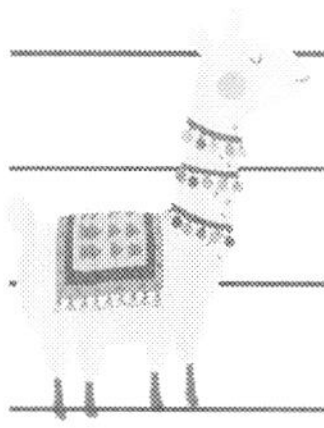

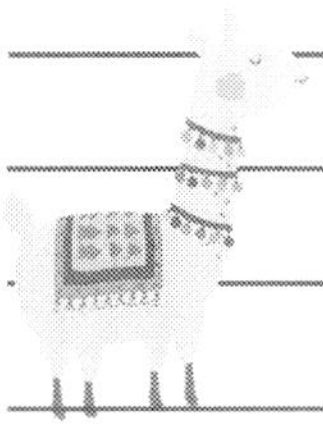

In case no one told you today -
You are LLamazing!

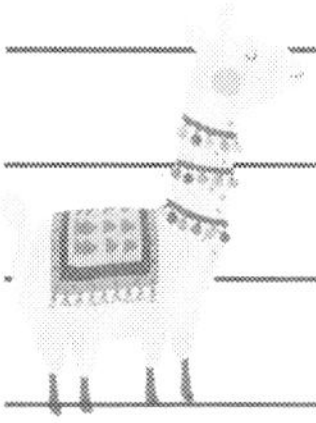

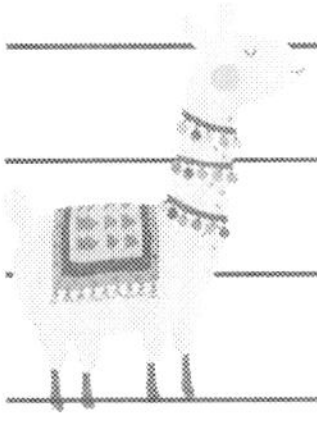

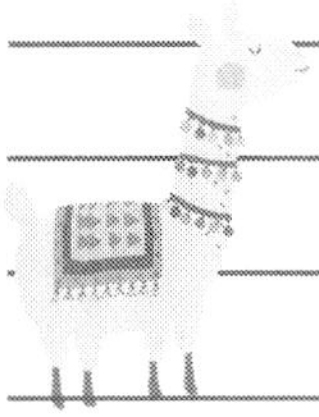

No act of kindness, no matter how small, is ever wasted.

– Aesop

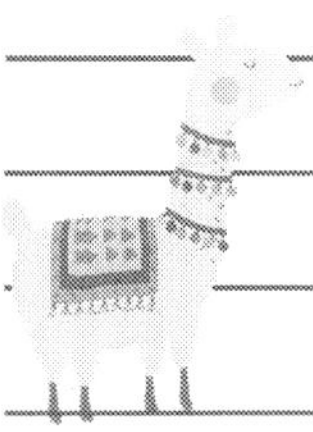

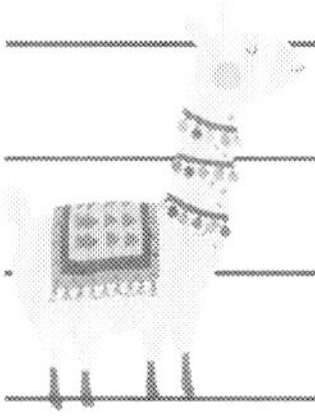

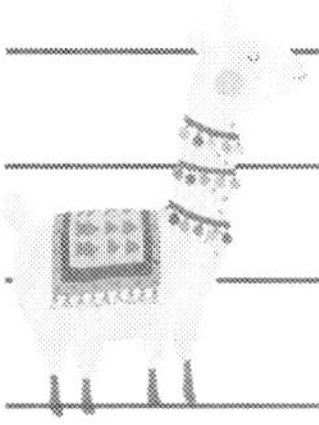

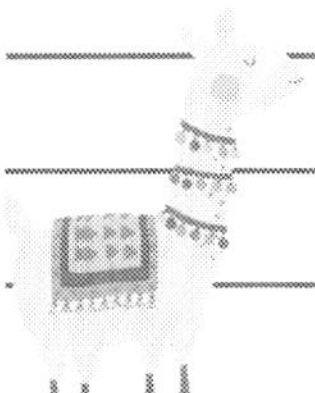

LLeave a LLitle sparkle wherever you go.

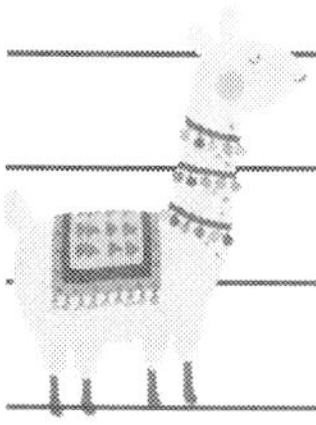

Be happy for this moment. This moment is your life.

– Omar Kayyam

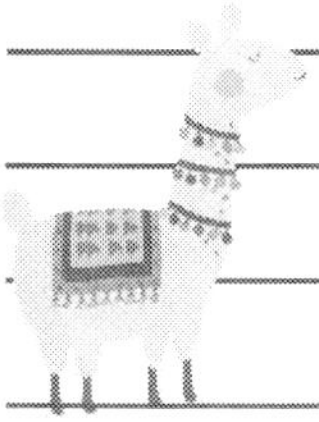

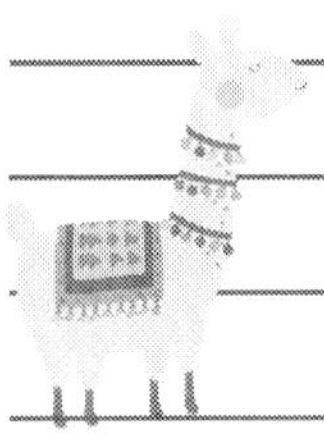

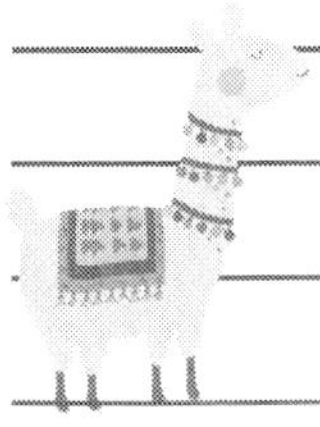

Peace is always beautiful.

– Walt Whitman

The greatest mistake you can make in life is to be continually fearing you will make one.

– Elbert Hubbard

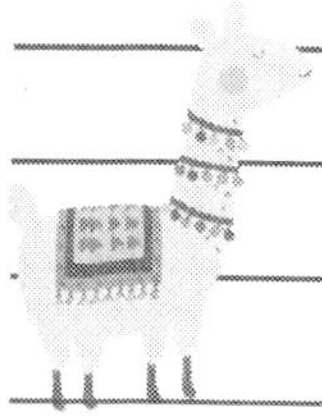

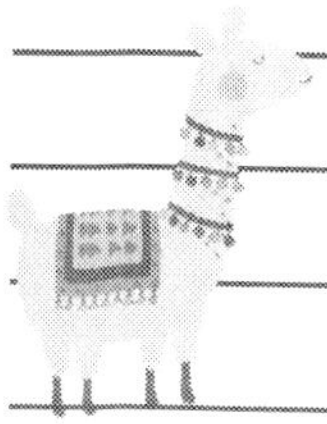

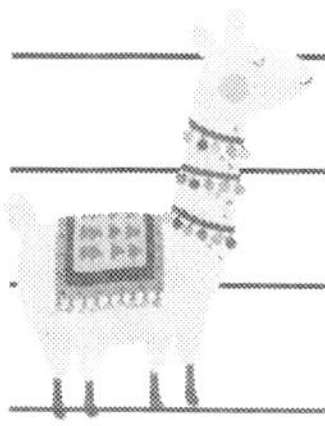

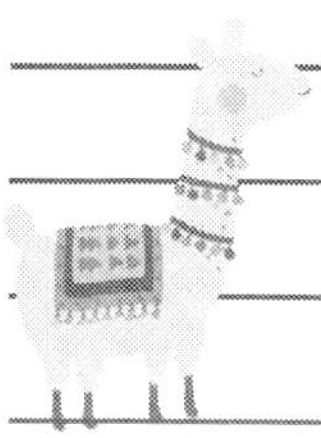

Bloom where you are planted.

- 1 Corinthians KJV

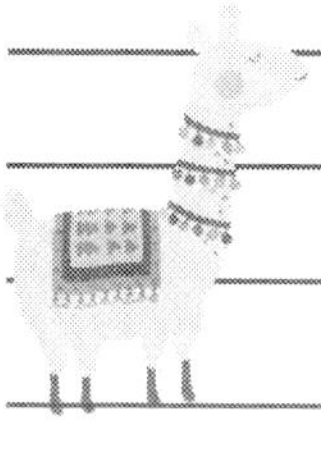

Made in the USA
Columbia, SC
12 December 2019

84754785R00054